The Art of Letting Go

Learning to Love Myself Through Poems of
Betrayal, Healing, and Forgiveness

Dedicated to my parents:
I've spent my life searching for a love like yours.

When a person decides to become a writer, they compromise their privacy. The sense of ownership that comes with certain mediums, such as diaries and journals, is taken away once you choose to go public. *Your memories no longer belong to you,* your words are an open field, accessible to all who are curious enough to read or listen. A writer has to be willing to share his or her work, and sometimes even go unrecognized for the sake of the art. I've come across my words on Facebook statuses and Instagram pages – on accounts of people I know, and those I've never seen before. Almost instinctively, I would become upset. My thoughts, my words, my feelings – were being praised and my name was nowhere to be found. Since then, I've been very selective about what I post and share... until a recent conversation gave me a change of heart: Writing is not about acknowledgement. It is about inspiring... causing somebody else to think, feel, or question something they haven't before. Taking the reader to a place as real as your mind is.

I have a confession: I've been holding out on you.

In this book you'll be able to follow the twists and turns of my love life – which at one point, I *thought* revolved around my partner. You'll be able to identify my mistakes and failures, like breaking someone's heart because I was unable to mend my own, and attracting unfit people into my life because that is exactly how I felt inside: like an unfit mess. Everything is intertwined – how I treated myself affected how I allowed others to treat me. My mental health affected the types of partners I constantly chose. You'll be able to identify the many emotions I experienced: anger, denial, resentment, exhaustion, and then nothing at all.

My very first pieces were a product of my bottled up feelings being triggered by a poem, book, or song, and exploding. I've added a few pages for notes throughout the book. Use them. Read. Feel. And Write. Don't explode.

—MP Frias

Love and loss are both travesties and blessings:

Through heartache, we all often lose ourselves. We forget that heartbreak - as much as love - is a personal journey we must all endure to truly uncover our strength. When we go through such despair, we fixate on the lover - the external source which submerges us into complete chaos. The pain that he or she has inflicted on us becomes the main character in our story. The anger. The resentment. The betrayal. The dismissive attitudes and bad intentions start to take center stage as our identities begin to wither away. These works are meant to challenge that notion. The antagonist is no longer in the spotlight feasting on our worth. These works are meant to reclaim our identities. The light is re-adjusted onto ourselves. Our emotional enlightenment. Our growth.

We come to the revelation that it was never about them.

—Daniela Mariot

Part One:
Loving You

Nobody knew you
quite like I did.
That's why they didn't understand.

How you hugged me
from behind,
or how you looked
while you were asleep.

They only saw your mistakes.

I've experienced your happiness,
your vulnerability, your pain,
and your desperation.
And felt each moment
as if it was happening to me.

My loyalty was my poison.

Constantly thinking:
"God wouldn't put you in my life
just to take you away."

A connection this powerful deserved a happy ending.

—Denial

"I love you," he says,
as he waits patiently for a reaction.

I stare blankly ahead, almost looking through flesh –
arbitrarily blurt out "I love you, too,"
and continue my absent gaze.

It was not a lie. I do love him,
But, I was lost in thought:

Do people ever change?
They obviously grow.
Adjusting to any alterations in their reality.
But over the years,
very particular actions stay the same.
Their mannerisms are unaffected,
laughter has not evolved.

And that's when it hit me...
That's who he is
and who he will always be:
The person that says "I love you"
only to hear it back.

—*Ulterior Motives*

I'm tired of celebrating whenever we go a day without arguing.
I'm tired of constantly feeling regret,
and regret, and regret,
and guilt.

I am tired of convincing myself to stay.

—*Exhaustion*

Your cell phone rang, and you said you didn't know who was calling.

An hour later I'm guessing passcodes while you're in the shower.

Skimming every name and stopping at the unfamiliar ones.
I even read the conversation with your best friend –
who I don't completely trust.
Constantly whispering to myself "stop looking for something you don't want to find," but unable to follow my own advice. It was addicting – like a part of me wanted to come across something terrible.

The water stopped running and I jumped up,
unsatisfied,
trying to put everything back in its place.

I'll try again tomorrow.

—*Confessions of an Insecure Girlfriend*

I want to hate you
and never look your way again.
Instead,
I text "get home safely."
Knowing very well
you don't deserve my worries.

I want to take everyone's advice
and give you up.
Instead,
I hold your head on my chest
and sleep in your arms.
Knowing very well
I'm not the only one.

—*Ignorance is Bliss*

Deep down,
I know you're not the problem.

You're just another victim
of his deceiving eyes
and pretty lies.

But somehow,
you're still the one I hate.

—*The Other Woman*

Betrayal promotes insecurities.
It wasn't about you anymore.
It was about me.

I kept thinking of what I did,
or could've done,
in order to make us work.

I'll ask you one last time:
What does she have that I don't?

—Blame

You would watch me cry,
and feel immediate guilt.

I wiped the tears
off your face,
before I wiped my own.

—*Priorities*

My arms wrapped
around his neck,
though every fiber of my being
knows they don't belong.

I bite his lips with anger,
and think of your face.

I just want to hurt you,
the way you hurt me.

—*Cheaters*

How is it possible to spend your life destroying
everything in front of you,
but a scratch hurts you so deeply?

Monsters should have thicker skin.

—Hypocrisy

There's a storm in my mind
that keeps me up at night,
and I stay awake
in hopes
that one day it will calm.

I always fall for potential.

I am sick of trying to explain
something I don't fully understand.
It was simply an irrational chapter
in the story of an extremely rational woman.

I was in love with who I wanted you to be
and obsessed with what we could be.

I always fall for potential.

—*Possibilities*

Notes

I already expect the worst.

I am emotionally drained,
and physically exhausted.

Nothing you do can surprise me.

—*Numb*

It was not your fault.

You should take *some* responsibility, though...

You have to understand that a person's mind is their most powerful adversary. It can play the role of an ally or a rival – and at that point in time, it was your *enemy.*

It was not your fault.

The first time it happened, you swore you'd forgive and forget. And I'll admit it – you made some honest attempts... you really did. But that's the main problem with thoughts: they're snowballs. Something so minuscule and seemingly anachronistic, feeds off of a faint emotion and slowly drives you insane. Eating away at any slight chance of happiness. Not returning a phone-call or breakfast with a friend is escalated into imaginary scenarios...

It was not your fault.

You tried to change. Minimized the sarcastic remarks, the arguments and 'I don't believe you's.' But it was too late; you were both already damaged beyond repair.

Thanks to that wicked mind of yours.

—*Resentment*

I stare right through you,
attempting to hide the emotion
from my face-
but you know me too well.

You ask me again:
"what's wrong?"

I have so much to say,
yet my lips refuse to move.

—*I'm Okay*

I've never been a fan of maybes.
Uncertainty never sat well with me,
and doubt casts a heavy feeling
in my stomach.

If you're going to leave,
I need you to leave
for good.

—Locked Door

On Monday,
I read through your emails
while you were in the shower.

On Thursday,
I checked your text messages
as you slept.

On Saturday,
I scrolled through every picture
you had saved on your phone.

I don't even know what I'm looking for.
I don't even know who I am anymore.

I just know
that this week
has been exhausting.

—Out of Character*

*Someone recently told me that "love makes you crazy," and I have to say I disagree. Love isn't possessive, controlling, or jealous. Love respects boundaries and finds trusting someone, easy. We have to stop glorifying unhealthy relationships. No, it doesn't mean they love you too much – it means they need help.

Everyone knows
that the longer you hold on,
the more difficult it is to let go.

It's been too long.

I am sick of sharing a room
with every doubt we've ignored,
and sharing a bed
with every argument we've had.

I always have to remind myself that
you can't fuck me into staying.

—*The Last Time*

"I can't do this anymore," she said. All in one breath – as if it was painful for her to say it so she rushed the words out of her mouth in order to calm the sting.

—*Without Flinching*

I pity the woman that tries to love him after me.

The dreaded sound of my name will eat her up inside. She will never be able to wear certain scents, say certain words. She will carry a list of places that she will not dare step foot in, because they have already been tainted with our laughter.

She will regretfully listen to stories of our remarkable romance and watch his eyes light up as he reminisces. She will probably never receive one of his hand written love letters. There will always be an inexplicably empty feeling when they're quiet in a room together.

It will be difficult for her to pretend like she didn't hear him *almost* say my name. *She will be in constant competition with my shadow*, knowing that the man that stands in front of her is the man that I helped mold.

The perks of being his first love: when he kisses her, they *both* have me on their mind.

—*Forever Number Two**

*This is the first piece I ever wrote. I read a poem by Clementine Von Radic and decided to mold it with my own heartache.

Can you ever feel the same love twice?

Are there stages? Like steps of a ladder.
Once you *love* – you *hurt* – you *learn*;
and next time you know better.

Leaving that last level to be eternally stored,
reserved;
ready to interrupt the next moment of temporary déjà vu.
Hindering your complete attachment –
constant reminders and "*remember what happened last time*"s.

Or maybe,
that intense mind-consuming,
anxiety-provoking,
instant mood-changing, blindness,
is a condition that *can* be repeated.

**It's years later and somebody makes you feel sixteen
again.**

The thought that there is no other love like your first is a bit
pessimistic. I agree, your first love is the most genuine, the most
pure. Your vulnerability makes it sincere. Your racing thoughts
make it exciting. Your daydreams make it real. But, if it is not
recurring, then **what is the point?** Why continue dating or
building relationships if nothing will ever compare to those vivid
teenage memories? Every other connection after those short-lived
months or years as a child, will seem dull and mediocre.

Granted, there is a concrete distinction between your first love and
every other dating experience after that.

Your first love is memorable, but will never measure up to the authenticity, security, and maturity of an adult relationship.
What was once infatuation later transforms into truly caring for somebody. Reliance becomes a co-dependency.

Think about it, do you honestly crave those rudimentary feelings back?

Undeveloped emotions, temporary insanity...

I guess the question isn't if you can ever feel the same love twice – rather, **would you want to?**

Once you *love* – you *hurt* – you *learn*; and next time you *know better.*

—*Just Once*

After years of studying
the rhythm
of your heartbeat,
you tell me to focus on a new topic.

After years of memorizing
every inch of your skin,
I am forced
to find a different muse.

Well, I have news for you...

After years of engraving
passion
with my nails
on your back

I've realized,
your scars will not heal overnight either.

—*Payback*

I don't forget.

Forgetting is not something you do,
it's something that happens.

And by the time you realize its occurrence,
you're back at square one.

—Try Again

I've always put your happiness before mine.

But, I refuse to be the bigger person
if that means I'm forced to smile
when I see you with
someone else.

—*Call Me Selfish*

I wish I was able to
forget your laugh,
and unlearn how you kiss.

I prefer to wipe my mind
and mouth
clean of all memory of you.

Because you can't miss what
you don't know you're missing.

—*Amnesia*

I have some good days.
When my job,
my friends,
and my life,
force me to forget.

And some bad days:
When a smell,
or a word,
triggers my memory.

I just pray that for once
the latter is outweighed.

—*Relapse*

I hope she ignores your messages
and steps all over your heart.

—*12 word story*

I wanted you.

To a point that I would
forgive,
and accept
and ignore
until I couldn't anymore.

At least we both know I tried.

—Breaking Point

I walk as far away as I can
and purge every map I have,
promising myself some unfamiliar ground.

I spend my days exploring,
yet somehow – end up at your door

—Roads

Notes

I like first dates.
I crave the nervousness that disappears once you get comfortable.
When your fingers accidentally touch and you quickly pull back;
half apologetic, half curious.

I am consumed with the thought of getting to know someone
for who they decided to be that morning,
without any interference from their past.

The stage where you're not focused on who's in front of you
but what made them that way.

I want to hear your side of every single story, so I'd be biased.
I want to have no reason not to trust you.

—*The Blank Slate*

'I have a vacant heart you can live in,'
I offered,
hinting at my inability to feel.

I never expected you to say 'so do I.'

Now here we are:
Two incomplete people,
destined to spend the rest of our
lives trying to repair each other.

I finally found someone
as damaged as I am,
but what good are two empty souls?

—*My Equal*

Every time I begin to trust someone,
they disappoint me.

You are no different –
as much as you say you are.
That's why I make sure to guard myself
above all else.

There is something so satisfying
about loving someone
with one foot out the door.

—*I'm Not Crazy, I'm Broken*

Concomitant with my need for romance
is a desire for roughness.
Nothing violent, but someone with a spine.

Someone who knows when to
delicately tuck my hair behind my ear,
and when to *pull it.*
When to gently kiss my lips
and when to bite my neck.

Someone who's conscious of the right time
to hold my hand,
and when to tie it behind my back.

Take me to a place where we only hear
the *succinct gasps* of enjoyable choking.
Where taking out your anger is encouraged.

Too much or too little
of either
will result in disinterest.
Nothing violent, but someone with a spine.

—Balance

Every time you leave,
you leave –
something behind
for me to pick up.

Resentment,
insecurity,
jealousy,
depression –
you know I'll be holding on
until I break.

Then I'll pick it up,
and carry it
to my next relationship.

—*Baggage*

I can see right through you–
loving and missing me
when it's convenient,
but unavailable when it's the other way around.

And though I know it's wrong:
I always pick up your call,
and always respond to your texts –

I am always the person
I wish you could be
for me.

While, in return,
you only pull me back in
once you think I might be
holding on to someone else.

You've been the toughest habit to break.

—*Taking Advantage*

After months of observing you,
I easily mastered how to make anyone
feel like they're the only one.

I immersed myself in my work,
As if my mind had to make up for my heart's inactivity.

Then, gained the trust of a person
with a heavy past and an unstable future.
Someone inexperienced cannot pry apart
who I am with who I pretend to be.

Finally, once I've consumed their sanity,
and they've absorbed my cynical ways –
I leave them with a burning desire
to do the same to someone else.

—*The Cycle*

I will make your mother love me,
and turn your sister into my best friend.

My plan is to upset you, test your patience,
and convince you to question your religion.
I will make you trust again,
even after you've sworn off love.

Then, tear down all the walls you built before me,
only to have them reconstructed *when I leave.*

—*Intentions*

There's a fine line
between privacy and secrecy.

We fall asleep in each other's arms,
just to sneak back
into the public eye
alone.

I've ended us in my mind
a million times.

But whenever our lips touch,
and our bodies meet,
the same question repeats
in my head:
Can love exist without witnesses?

—Confidential

You deserve better.

You deserve someone stable,
someone sane,
someone open to love.
I can't be that for you right now.

I am too cynical,
too hurt –
too broken.

Let's not do this.
One of us will lose,
and this time
it won't be me.

—Rebound

"I don't want a relationship"
ultimately means
"I don't want *you*."

—*Hidden Messages*

We were over in your mind
Before it was ever a reality.

Even when we hugged;
I felt like I was holding on
for my life,
while you were slowly releasing.

—The First Step

Guilty because even though I love you,
I know I'm not in love with you.
Guilty because even though I am happy,
I know this has an expiration date.
Guilty because every time I consider
choosing you,
I remember
that you deserve someone
who doesn't have to second guess.

—*Waste of Time*

After sleepless nights,
I've decided
that we cannot be together.

It is unfair of me to take responsibility
for someone else's happiness,
when I can't even control
my own.

—*Unstable*

I remember when your eyes
used to
follow me across a room,
now they squint at the sound of my name.
Almost as if verbalizing my person
inflicts physical pain.

—I'm Sorry

Have you ever felt stuck?
Watching the days go by,
unable to distinguish one from another.
Routine is mental suicide.

There's a difference between being alive and living.
The latter requires effort, excitement,
and something new to look forward to.

I need a reason to continue doing this.

—*Quicksand*

Isn't it crazy how
our unconscious bodies
still find each other at night.

—*Cravings*

Insomnia took over at night.

I used to stare at the ceiling
and think of every reason I have
to stick by your side.

Once we went our separate ways,
I wrote down every reason I had
to not get back with you.

That piece of paper will outlast our memories.
Soon I'll be able to sleep just fine.

—*Set in Stone*

I remember it vividly:
you apologized as tears flooded your eyes,
looking down at your hands the entire time.

You said you were sorry.

You said you didn't mean to ruin this.

You said you learned your lesson.

I believed you –
but that doesn't mean we should be together.
I am done giving people chances to hurt me.

—Enough

I've been trying so hard to make these words
more beautiful than what they really are.
Intense, instead of apathetic.
Passionate as opposed to empty.
Its purpose was to stimulate feeling, any feeling.

For now I'll just stick to the truth – I'm terrified.
I am not sure if my past has scarred me to a point of numbness,
or if I am subconsciously, yet consciously,
stalling my complete emotional involvement.
Not only in a relationship, but in anything and everything I do.

It took me two full weeks to cry.

I used to just lie on a disheveled bed
and stare at the ceiling; detached.
Unable to think, and less able to sleep.

Eight months later I can see the difference:
something is inside of me that was not there before,
or something that was there, is missing.
I am not quite sure which of the two it is.

—*Visual Heartbreak*

I just needed you to fight for me.

Instead, you said
you understood
and kept walking.

You make moving on look so easy.

It made me question
how deeply this affected you,
or if it did,
at all.

I should've let you leave months ago.

—*Retrospect*

An open letter to every man I've ever loved:

Dear Stranger,

I loved you when I was sure I would never love again. However, each time was a different kind of love. Regardless of the type, they were all equally as life-changing.

Every man that I've ever loved has been the same person: sarcastic, ambitious, and stubborn. A man so incredibly blinded by the thought of success, that his tunnel-vision caused him to over-look the small advantages that he's received. Never satisfied with his winnings; always with a relentless hunger for more. I've always thought of you as a reflection of myself because at some point in time, you showed me both who I ought to be and who I refused to become. On one hand, I admire you: A person who is so incredibly drowned in his work, that he sometimes forgets to come up for air. At the same time, however, I detested being numbers 3 and 4 on your list of priorities.

You were selfish. *I wanted to fix you.*

I became absorbed by your demeanor and consumed by your character. In exchange, you assimilated my code of ethics and mentality into your life. I became you, and you became me. In the process of finding you, however, I lost myself.

Our timing was off.
The problem with relationships is that there is *no such thing* as starting fresh. You transport all the luggage from your previous affairs into this new connection and whether you like it or not, your perception is altered. After some time, I came to the conclusion that I could break my own heart – I didn't need your help.

Though I am no longer the person who runs her fingers through your hair, or the woman who sits with you in the car at 11pm listening to you detach yourself from the heaviness of your day, I will always be here. I am going to live in your innermost thoughts. I will turn your mirror into my home and always reemerge just when you think I've entirely departed.

Keep making me proud, keep making yourself proud.

Ps. If you think I am writing about you, I am.

Notes

Part Two:
Loving Myself

It was obvious that we were
draining one another.
Something that started out so strong,
eventually diminished after weeks of
trying,
and giving up,
and trying some more.

As the disagreements increased,
our loving moments
came few and far between.

I had to choose between
loving you
or loving myself.

I made the right decision.

—*The Break-Up*

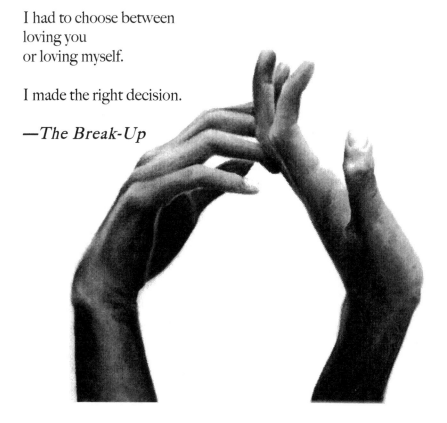

Love is not enough.

If it isn't accompanied
by trust, respect, and support,
I don't want it.

—*Standards*

It's too bad you couldn't convince me to stay.
It's too bad you didn't try to.

—*Mutual Agreement*

I sometimes wish that I was able
to hold on to grudges;
Instead, I easily forgive people
who do not deserve forgiveness.

Once you left, my thoughts became
permanently redesigned to second guess.
I quickly realized that a damaged mind
can never return to sanity.

Misused by experience
and destroyed by suspicion.
You flooded my memories
and ruined my expectations.

Forgiving is effortless.
Forgetting is exhausting.

—Scarred

I miss the old me.
The one who laughed loudly
and trusted openly.

I don't want you back,
I want myself back.

—*Lost*

You showed me how little I meant,
and I did everything I could
to change your mind.

I desperately needed
you to see my worth.

Blaming your betrayal on myself.

When in reality,
your lack of maturity
had nothing to do
with me.

—*Your Fault*

You're everywhere.
In my favorite sweater,
and in the movie I watched last night.
In rainy days, and scenic views.

But sometimes,
you're in places you shouldn't be.
Like in my bed at 3 in the morning
when I can't fall asleep -
or on the tip of my tongue
every time I orgasm.

Your ghost is difficult to ignore
and impossible to forget.
I don't think I want to.

—The Haunting

I painted our names on your skin
with my fingertips,
and carved 'forever' on your back
with my nails.

In pictures, we're still happy.
In letters, we're still together.

With art we lived,
and through art we'll continue.

—*Masterpiece*

Nothing I say will ever be enough.
They're all lies created to soothe your reality.

Every "it'll be okay,"
is only insulting to your intelligence.
Every "you'll be fine,"
is hurting you a little more.

I just want your pain to go away.

—*Quiet**

*This was written for a friend who recently lost her father.
Sometimes, words aren't necessary. People might just need
you to be there and share the silence.

I've been avoiding my notebook
for quite some time now.

Terrified of my craft...
Which is beautiful once complete,
but draining on your way there.

Writing is reliving,
and I don't have the strength
to carry the same heaviness twice.

After hours of staring at an empty page,
I quickly scribbled one sentence:
You're lucky if you can't relate to this.

—The Broken Artist

Men become a collection
of the women that love them.

Their personality is adapted from
past experiences,
stitched together with nothing
but good intentions
and disappointments.

But as I piece you together, I tear myself apart.

My fixing days are over.
It's finally time to work on myself.

—One Sided

It takes me back.

As soon as the scent finds my nose,
I am prompted with instant disgust.
Memories of exhaustion,
regret,
and anger.

I stay away from roses now.

What they do overweighs
what they are.

Whoever you choose to love,
I hope they don't ruin flowers for you.

—Flashbacks

I *accidentally* think about him
on cloudy days,
because they remind me
how much he hates the rain.

It was the one thing capable of surprising him,
regardless of how many times he was warned.

I always had to make sure
he grabs an umbrella
"just in case."

The words were not enough.
He had to feel the drops falling on his head
in order to believe the weather.

I was an optimist and he was a realist.

A year later,
after each cloudy noon,
all day drizzles and midnight storms,
hurricanes and morning rain showers,
And after every *accidental* thought;

I've realized that
I am in love with memories,
not him,
and I really hope he doesn't forget his umbrella.

—*The Realist*

I store my feelings
in a locked jar
to keep them from spilling.

There is no middle ground:
I am either burning flames
or wet matches.

I've come to the conclusion that
I'd rather be numb than in pain;
And it's probably for the best,
because everybody knows
that you can't cool down a fire.

—Closed In

It's obvious that I didn't mean anything
to you.
None of this would be happening if I did.

Someone that cares about another person
wouldn't do everything in their power to destroy them.
They wouldn't build up their dreams,
just to slowly
tear them apart
one
by
one.

Someone that cares about another person
wouldn't watch their world collapse
and do nothing
to prevent it.

—*Realization*

I've always been the type to
talk someone off a ledge,
while my world is collapsing
beneath me.

Constantly bestowing advice
that I am unable to practice
myself.

Spreading positivity;
focusing on my words,
but ignoring their source.

—*Selfless*

I have some good days.
When my job,
my friends,
and my life
force me to forget.

And some bad days:
When a smell,
or a word,
triggers my memory.

I just pray that for once
the latter is outweighed.

—In Time

Basic human interactions
aren't satisfying my cravings.

I'm alone,
but accompanied
by your memory.

—*Missing*

Every day you showed me
that you didn't need me,
 and every day
I stuck around.

Not because I needed you –
because I needed
to prove you wrong.

—*Worth*

I always knew
you would leave.

I just wish
you would've taken
our memories
with you.

—*Insomnia*

I tried to make your memory
background noise,
But the constant thought of you
is deafening.

I never want to see you again,
yet I crave you more than ever.

But I will not
walk backwards
any longer.

It's like relighting a used candle.
Desperately trying
to salvage what was left
of us.

Attempting to bring back the light
that was blinding me
in the first place.

—Let Go

There are two types of rain:

The sudden storm,
when everything
falls on you at once.

And the all day drizzle.
When you feel like your pain
will never end.

Both equally
painful,
cleansing,
and
necessary.

—*Forecast*

Notes

Our time apart taught me a few things:

Never let the fear of being alone
push you to hold someone's hand.
They will never be enough.

Never allow another human
to satisfy your emptiness.
You will be twice as lost.

Never let the voices in your head
talk you into someone else's arms.
Their warmth will never comfort you.

You need to be whole on your own.

—*Guidelines*

I tried to ignore it,
but my dissatisfaction is so loud
it's deafening.

I've become obsessed with
the woman I am supposed to be.

She's the reason behind everything I do.
My actions are carefully executed
with that familiar face in mind.

I won't stop until I'm *her.*

—*Evolution*

There is nothing worse than a woman
who knows her worth.

Her laughter is as addicting as her kiss.
Her inviting eyes are never mentioned
without equal tribute to her intelligence and humor.

Though she carries the burden of being strong,
she walks at a lively pace,
with her hands in her pockets.

She is a journey to obtain,
a challenge to keep,
and a shame to lose.

She is me.
She is you.

—The Perfect Woman

We've been taught to glorify indifference;
the less you feel, the more you're admired.

But people who were dragged
into darkness,
and protected their light
are the ones we should look up to.

The ones who remained whole
even after believing
they were shattered.

Not those who whisper every 'I love you.'

—*The Real Heroes*

There are people that I cant live without,
but I don't show them I love them,
because I simply
don't know how.

—*Forgive Me*

I would easily trade a night on the town
for a night by your side.

Instead, I'm forcing conversations
and feigning contentment.

More memories with every sip.
Stronger feelings with every shot.

I drink to forget and the opposite occurs.

—*Drunk Dial*

I've spent days learning
to love myself-
and nights wishing
I had someone else's life.

I never learned
how to take a compliment,
and never learned
how to forget insults.

But, I've decided to change.
Negativity becomes reality
if you let it.

I refuse to let it.

—Insecurities

I saw you as a project.
Something I needed to fix.
You were a challenge,
and the prize would be taming you.

I spent years molding you,
teaching you right
from wrong,
showing you how to love-
and in exchange, I would be able to say:
"he changed for *me*."

"Because *I'm* so great...
and it took him a while,
but he sees that now."

I never got my wish.

Selfish choices are never rewarded.

—*Ego*

Don't flatter yourself.
You were the second person I called.

—I Don't Need You, I Just Need Someone

I keep my bed occupied
to help me forget how empty I am.

I thought I was craving the warmth
of a body next to mine,
but it's more than that.
It's your fingers running through
my hair
until I drift into sleep.
It's the squeeze you would give me
when you gained consciousness
in the middle of the night
and realized I was next to you.

Warmth simply
doesn't do that.

Instead, it reminds me that someone else
is laying on your side of the bed.
It gives me something to compare you to.
It leaves me unsatisfied.

—*Memory Loss*

I always considered
myself to be a very
strong woman,

until I found myself
searching for the strength
to keep him out.

—*Test*

I constantly tell myself:
"There is nothing
that time can't fix."

So I wait.

And I feel myself healing
from within.

—*Rebirth*

Sometimes, home
has eyes and a mouth.
Home hugs back
and listens-
and sometimes,
home changes location.

—*Soulmate*

Though at the time it didn't seem like the best idea, in retrospect, letting go was the best decision I've ever made. Every time he didn't pick up my call, I wrote. Every time I felt alone, I remembered that I created a world inside my head. Whenever I felt weak, I focused that strength on my work. Every time I cried myself to sleep, I woke up thankful. Every disappointment brought me to appreciate myself so much more. Though I thought you were hurting me, it was actually making me stronger. When you finally left, you forced me to love myself.

—*Thank You*

Before walking away,
he turned
and said,
"happiness looks good on you."

—*Better Apart*

Woman,
the world has made you stiff.
Confusing hardness for strength,
your inability to feel is considered
an ability to survive.

Haven't you heard?
You are able to cry, love,
and feel,
deeply –
and still be strong.

Your strength is not defined
by your emotions.

—*Being Human*

Everyone has always told me
that I am identical to my mother.
It took me years
to realize
they don't mean physically.

—Temperament

He held my hand tight-
but I was always unsure of whether
it was to guide me,
or to keep me from going anywhere.
He grabbed me by my waist,
but only when others were looking.
He told me he loved me,
and always waited for a response.

—Possession*

*"When you like a flower, you pluck it –
when you love a flower, you water it daily."

I walked by our favorite restaurant recently.
Butterflies rushed into my body,
and I shook them away as quickly
as they arrived.

That's when I realized:
you can miss someone
and still never want to see them again.

—*No Regrets*

I am so grateful for those who betrayed me.
The ones that smiled in my face,
and collected information
just to use it against me in the future.

I am so grateful for those who left me.
Those who didn't feed my need
for love, attention, or support.
Those who let me starve.

It all brought me where I am today:
eternally thankful.

—*What Doesn't Kill You*

Silly boys,
the simple fact that I am walking through
what you've claimed to be
your space,
is not an invitation to touch me.
My body is not public property.

Silly boys,
This morning,
as I pulled up my tight jeans,
let go of my hair,
and carefully painted on my face,
you were not on my mind.
I wanted to be beautiful for myself.

Silly boys,
telling me to smile,
or asking for a 'thank you,'
will not get a reaction out of me.
I do not owe you a thing.

—Reminder

When he found me, I was naive and curious. Ready to accept any rendition of love, even if it was not what I deserved. I lowered my standards and accepted more apologies than I could forgive. Mistaking obsession for love, while ignoring all the signs.

When you found me, I was nothing short of a wreck. Apathetic, damaged, and hurting. You somehow managed to love the darkest parts of me, with no hesitation - while giving me the peace of mind I craved. Our relationship eclipsed every past affair.

—Why I Love You More

My time is what I cherish most.
I'm selfish and selective –
wary of how I spend it,
and with whom.

I don't think you understand
how lucky
you truly are.

—*Options*

Even if you aren't my queen –
you are somebody else's,
and you deserve to always
be treated like royalty.

—*Stranger*

Speak lightly,
my tongue was crafted
with Cleopatra's in mind.

I have the endurance of those before me
and my ancestor's power
flooding my veins.

Falling a million times,
I'll get up a million and one.

I am indestructible.

—*Destiny*

I hope that one day you fall so deep in love,
you'll laugh at your past romances...
realizing how insignificant they were.

I hope that one day you crawl into bed,
stare at the ceiling,
and feel completely at peace with where you are in life.

I hope that you give the world everything you have to offer.
I hope that your absence is always louder than your presence.

I just want you to know that this is all worth it.
Stop worrying about the destination –
the journey is more important.

—*A Letter to My Best Friend*

I'm sorry for highlighting your flaws
and overlooking your strengths.

I'm sorry for feeding your insecurities
and starving your ego.

I'm sorry for being your worst enemy;
always there to criticize,
never around to encourage.

I'm sorry for not calling you
intelligent, beautiful, and worthy –
every single day.

—*Conversations with the Mirror*

An open letter to every woman I've ever loved:

Dear Stranger,

Every woman I've ever loved has *become* the same person: intelligent, captivating, and addicting. Starting out as a beautiful young girl who had more love than you knew what to do with. Your main problem was that you'd easily add another person into your already overflowing heart, and always forget to leave space for yourself. I've been there. I understand.

You tried to keep yourself busy, in fear that free time will one day be equivalent to an emotional break-down. You worked too much, studied too much, trained too much, and didn't sleep enough. Spent your days surrounded by meaningless chatter in hopes that it will drown out the voices in your head.
But then night would come, and you'd be forced to face your feelings.

That's when you realized that running from yourself was an impossible task. And you finally understood the meaning of the saying "when it rains, it pours."

You are my favorite because you never let heartbreak compromise your character. You turned negativity into motivation and loneliness into fearlessness. I'm glad you realized that you will never fully satisfy a man who doesn't know what he wants. I'm even happier to see that you've finally made yourself number one in your life. You ultimately transformed from a smart, yet naïve, young girl into a focused, outspoken, beast of a woman. Keep making me proud, keep making yourself proud.

Love always,
mp

Ps. If you think I'm writing about you, I am.

Dedicated to Massiel, Jamie, Amy, and Kat - my rocks.

Notes

Notes

Notes

Notes

Author Contact:

web: mpfrias.com
email: info@mpfrias.com
instagram: @mp.frias
twitter: @friasmp
hashtag: #mpfrias

Illustrator Contact:

email: daniela.mariot28@gmail.com
instagram: @danielamariot
twitter: @danielamariot
hashtag: #danielamariot

The Scarlet Event Contact:

web: mpfrias.com/scarlet
email: thescarletevent@gmail.com
instagram: @thescarletevent
hashtag: #thescarletevent

Thank you for believing in me.

34466597R00073

Made in the USA
Middletown, DE
22 August 2016